This book belongs to

KLM Publishing
Longview, TX

www.klmpublish.com

Names: Miller, Kari (Kari Leigh), author. | Ribeiro, Leticia, illustrator.
Title: I do not like peas / written by Kari Miller ; illustrated by Leticia Ribeiro.
Description: Longview, TX : KLM Publishing, [2023] | Audience: children/early readers. | Summary: "I do not like peas" is a lighthearted story about a little girl who is faced with an all too common predicament. She absolutely does not want to eat her peas, so she begins to think of all the ways she could wish them away and make them disappear. This is a humorous tale that most children and even adults can relate to which makes it a fun book for parents to read to their little ones and young readers to enjoy.--Publisher.
Identifiers: ISBN: 979-8-9876034-1-3 (paperback) | 979-8-9876034-0-6 (hardcover) | 979-8-9876034-2-0 (ebook) | LCCN: 2023921897
Subjects: LCSH: Peas--Juvenile fiction. | Likes and dislikes--Juvenile fiction. | Vegetables--Juvenile fiction. | Imagination--Juvenile fiction. | Obstinacy--Juvenile fiction. | Girls--Psychology-- Juvenile fiction. | Child psychology--Juvenile fiction. | Humorous stories. | Children's stories. | CYAC: Peas--Fiction. | Likes and dislikes--Fiction. | Vegetables--Fiction. | Imagination-- Fiction. | Obstinacy--Fiction. | Girls--Psychological aspects--Fiction. | Humorous stories. | LCGFT: Humorous fiction.
Classification: LCC: PZ7.1.M5814 I13 2023 | DDC: [E]--dc23

Book Design by Arlene Soto, Intricate Designs.

With contributions by Morgan Miller Rodgers for the original character design.

I Do NOT Like Peas

written by **Kari Miller**

illustrated by **Leticia Ribeiro**

"Porgy," called Mom, "dinner's now on your plate."
It all smelled so good; Porgy hardly could wait.
Was it pasta and meatballs or chicken and rice?

Tacos with cheese and some beans would be nice!

The night before, Mom made a tender pot roast,
with creamy potatoes and hot buttered toast.

Porgy raced to the table and sat in her seat,
Then grabbed up her spoon and fork, ready to eat!

But what happened next was a total surprise,
In fact, Porgy couldn't believe her own eyes!

Little green balls, maybe seven or eight,
sat next to her chicken Mom put on her plate.

She stared at her dinner and then looked at her mom,
She took a deep breath and she tried to stay calm.

Fork in her hand, Porgy poked one or two.
"Try them," Mom urged her. "Porgy, they're so good for you.

Green peas are quite tasty, they're ever so small.
If you eat them all, they will help you grow tall."

Porgy decided that she would taste one.
She'd chew it up fast and then she would be done.

The green pea was little, what Mom said was right.
It squished in her mouth when she took her first bite.

She knew right away what she feared had come true.
She hated these peas, but now, what could she do?

She sipped on her water and picked at her meat,
eyeing the peas Mom had told her to eat.

If only Mom gave me a dog when I asked,
then he'd eat my peas—they would disappear fast!

Then Mom would think it was little ol' me,
who ate every single last little green pea.

But there was no dog, she could not share her peas.
They sat on her plate, as Mom said, "Porgy, please!"

She squeezed her eyes tight, and she wished them away,
but the peas, she soon saw, seemed to be there to stay.

If I were a **wizard**, she thought to herself,
I'd pick a "pea potion" from my potion shelf.

I'd sprinkle my peas when my mom was not near,
to make every one of these peas disappear.

Or what if an army of **ants** happened by
each one in a line, with their heads all held high.

If they'd be so kind as to each take a pea,
the peas would be gone before my mom could see!

Then Porgy remembered a story she'd read,
About tiny **fairies** with crowns on their heads.

*I wish that a fairy would visit me now,
she'd carry the peas off, I'm sure she'd know how!*

She sat there so long that the peas grew quite cold.

She sighed, for she knew she must do as Mom told.

By then, Mom was rinsing her own dinner plate.
She had to act fast, she could no longer wait.

She rolled a few peas on her plate 'til one **squished**,
and right then she knew how to get what she wished.

She held her fork tight and she mashed the peas flat,
her bread went on top, and then that was just that!

Porgy felt sneaky; she felt rather clever.
Would Mom catch her trick?

Oh, no way!

She would **NEVER!**

At school the next day, Porgy opened her lunch:
A sandwich, some crackers, and white cheese to munch.

Then lifting her napkin, she saw a small note.
It came from her mother, and here's what she wrote:

My dear, darling Porgy, I do hope you know,
I love you so dearly and want you to grow.

I packed you a sandwich and gave you some cheese,
And there's a surprise, it's a few yummy peas!

But please, Porgy, don't mash your peas up today!
I found all the dinner peas you hid away.

Porgy thought her plan was the best one ever.
But she learned that day that Mom was **ALSO** clever!

Meet the Author!

What do you get when you take a shy redheaded girl from Longview, Texas, give her a passion for writing at age eleven, and add a rib-tickling sense of humor? **That would be Kari Miller!**

Kari grew up with her younger twin sisters. Adults would always ask, "Oh, I bet your sisters get all the attention because they are twins!" And Kari would look at them with her freckled face and reply, "Yes, but I have red hair, so it evens out." Most children simply want to fit in and look like their peers. Since only 1-2 percent of the world's population has red hair, that wasn't easy for Kari to do. Although her fiery red hair made her stand out, Kari mostly enjoyed writing alone in her bedroom.

By the time she graduated high school, she had accumulated pages and pages of short stories and poems, compiling them into small journals. Kari continued to write as an adult with her love of poetry and story telling only growing. Becoming a mother and raising her three children gave her a wealth of humorous tales to draw from. That, coupled with her own sweet memories of childhood provided more than enough content to create stories that she believes young children can relate to.

Writing for children is Kari's dream come true. Putting smiles on their faces and helping them see that we are all not so different is the cherry on top!

Meet the Illustrator!

Leticia Ribeiro is a Brazilian illustrator who is currently based in Ireland. At a young age, she developed a passion for drawing. When she moved to Ireland in 2017, a graphic artist noticed her work. Her interest then shifted from architecture to illustrations. After landing her first freelance job, she decided to pursue a career as an illustrator.

In 2022, she was nominated as one of the top ten finalists for the Penguin Publisher Cover Design Award. Leticia continues to work on multiple projects to sharpen her craft.

No peas were harmed in the making of this book!